Helen Exley Giftbooks
Thoughtful giving starts here...

OTHER HELEN EXLEY GIFTBOOKS:

Wisdom for the new Millennium
Words on Hope
Words on Love and Caring
Thank You for Every Little Thing

First published 1998. Published in this format 2001.
Copyright © Helen Exley 1998, 2001.
The moral right of the author has been asserted.

12 11 10 9 8 7 6 5 4 3 2 1

Edited and pictures selected by Helen Exley
ISBN 1-86187-290-9

Printed in China.

Exley Publications Ltd, 16 Chalk Hill, Watford,
Herts WD19 4BG, UK.
Exley Publications LLC, 232 Madison Avenue, Suite 1409,
NY 10016, USA.

Words on
CALM

A HELEN EXLEY GIFTBOOK

EXLEY
NEW YORK • WATFORD, UK

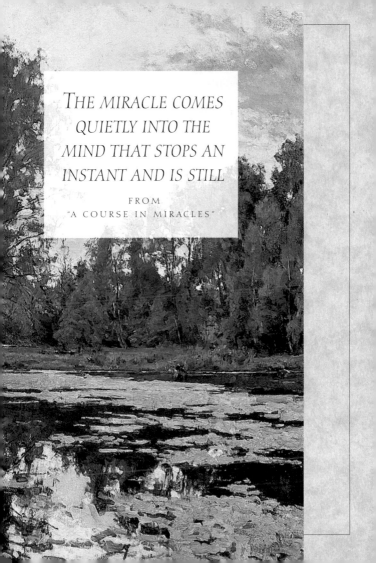

THE MIRACLE COMES
QUIETLY INTO THE
MIND THAT STOPS AN
INSTANT AND IS STILL

FROM
"A COURSE IN MIRACLES"

Contentment...
comes as the infallible
result of great
acceptances, great
humilities –
of not trying to make
ourselves this or that
(to conform
to some dramatized
version of ourselves),
but of surrendering
ourselves to the
fullness of life –
of letting life
flow through us.

DAVID GRAYSON

*W*hy should we live with such hurry and waste of life? ... Men say that a stitch in time saves nine, and so they take a thousand stitches today to save nine tomorrow. As for work, we haven't any of any consequence. We have Saint Vitus' dance, and cannot possibly keep our heads still.

HENRY DAVID THOREAU
(1817-1862)

*L*isten in deep silence.
Be very still and open
your mind....
Sink deep into the peace that
waits for you beyond
the frantic, riotous thoughts
and sights and sounds
of this insane world.

FROM "A COURSE IN MIRACLES"

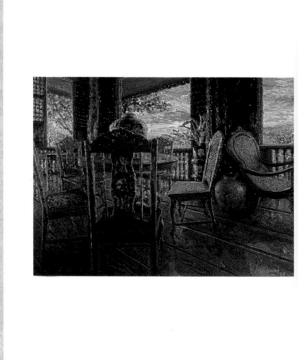

*S*erenity is neither
frivolity, nor complacency,
it is the highest knowledge
and love, it is the
affirmation of all reality
being awake at the edge
of all deeps and abysses.
Serenity is the secret
of beauty and the real
substance of all art.

HERMANN HESSE
(1877-1962)

THE SERENE

HAVE NOT OPTED OUT

OF LIFE.

THEY SEE MORE WIDELY,

LOVE MORE DEARLY,

REJOICE IN THE THINGS

THE FRANTIC MIND

NO LONGER SEES

OR HEARS.

PAM BROWN, b.1928

Leave home in the sunshine:

Dance through a meadow –

Or sit by a stream

and just be.

The lilt of the water

Will gather your worries

And carry them down

to the sea.

J. DONALD WALTERS

*Serenity does not
cancel hope or adventure,
work or love.
It flows through the landscape
of our busy lives,
quiet and strong.
Clear and gentle.
Refreshing all we do
or dream.*

PAM BROWN, b.1928

Work is not always required of a man. There is such a thing as sacred idleness, the cultivation of which is now fearfully neglected.

GEORGE MACDONALD (1824-1905)

IF YOU CAN SPEND A PERFECTLY USELESS AFTERNOON IN A PERFECTLY USELESS MANNER, YOU HAVE LEARNED HOW TO LIVE.

LIN YUTANG (1895-1976)

*P*eace is the
fairest form of
happiness.

WILLIAM ELLERY CHANNING
(1780-1842)

*Teach me the art
of creating islands
of stillness,
in which I can absorb
the beauty of
everyday things:
clouds, trees, a snatch
of music....*

MARION STROUD

Don't hurry don't worry,
you're only here
for a short visit.
So be sure to stop
and smell the flowers.

WALTER HAGAN

Whatever peace I know
rests in the natural world,
in feeling myself a part of it,
even in a small way.

MAY SARTON,
FROM "JOURNAL OF A SOLITUDE"

OUR GREATEST EXPERIENCES
ARE OUR QUIETEST MOMENTS.

NIETZSCHE
(1844-1900)

*Happiness is
as a butterfly, which,
when pursued, is always
beyond our grasp,
but which, if you will
sit down quietly, may alight
upon you.*

NATHANIEL HAWTHORNE
(1804-1864)

*The way to use life
is to do nothing
through acting. The way
to use life is to do
everything through being.*

LAO-TZU

Do not let trifles disturb your tranquillity of mind....
Life is too precious to be sacrificed for the nonessential and transient....
Ignore the inconsequential.

GRENVILLE KLEISER

*There is, perhaps,
no solitary sensation
so exquisite as that of
slumbering on the grass
or hay, shaded from
the hot sun by a tree,
with the consciousness
of a fresh light air
running through the
wide atmosphere,
and the sky stretching
far overhead
upon all sides.*

LEIGH HUNT
(1784-1859)

Deep in the soul, below pain,
below all the distraction of life,
is a silence vast and grand –
an infinite ocean of calm,
which nothing can disturb;
Nature's own exceeding peace,
which "passes understanding".
That which we seek with
passionate longing,
here and there, upward and
outward; we find at last
within ourselves.

C.M.C. QUOTED BY R.M. BUCKE

*There is no quiet place
in the white man's cities,
no place to hear the leaves
of spring or the rustle
of insects' wings....
The Indians prefer the soft
sound of the wind
darting over the face
of the pond, the smell
of the wind itself cleansed
by the midday rain,
or scented with pinion pine.*

CHIEF SEATTLE

Life just is. You have to flow with it. Give yourself to the moment. Let it happen.

GOVERNOR JERRY BROWN

*A*rranging a bowl
of flowers in the morning
can give a sense of quiet
in a crowded day –
like writing a poem,
or saying a prayer.

ANNE MORROW LINDBERGH

*Here will we sit
and let the sounds
of music creep in our ears:
soft stillness and the night
become the touches of
sweet harmony.*

WILLIAM SHAKESPEARE
(1564-1616)

*THE QUIETER
YOU BECOME,
THE MORE
YOU CAN HEAR.*

BABA RAM DASS

*If we are not happy,
if we are not peaceful,
we cannot share peace
and happiness with others,
even those we love, those
who live under the same roof.
If we are peaceful,
if we are happy, we can smile
and blossom like a flower,
and everyone in our family,
our entire society, will
benefit from our peace.*

THICH NHAT HANH

When I set myself sometimes
to consider the divers agitations
of men, and the troubles and
dangers to which they expose
themselves.... I see that all
their misfortunes come
from one thing only,
that they know not how
to dwell in peace,
in a room.

BLAISE PASCAL
(1623-1662)

*O*ver all the mountaintops

Is peace.

In all treetops

You perceive

Scarcely a breath.

The little birds in the forest

Are silent.

Wait then; soon

You, too, will have peace.

JOHANN WOLFGANG
VON GOETHE
(1749-1832)

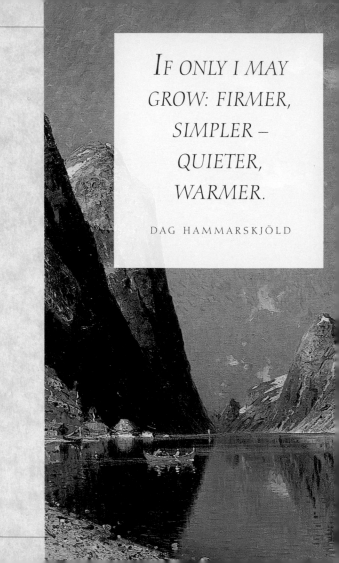

IF ONLY I MAY GROW: FIRMER, SIMPLER – QUIETER, WARMER.

DAG HAMMARSKJÖLD

I lay in a meadow
until the unwrinkled serenity
entered into my bones,
and made me into one
with the browsing kine,
the still greenery,
the drifting clouds,
and the swooping birds.

ALICE JAMES

I expand and live
in the warm day
like corn and melons.

RALPH WALDO EMERSON
(1803-1882)

Peace is not something you wish for; it's something you make, something you do, something you are, and something you give away!

ROBERT FULGHUM

Serenity is active.
It is a gentle and firm
participation with trust.
Serenity is the relaxation
of our cells into who we are
and a quiet celebration
of that relaxation.

ANNE WILSON SCHAEF

Peace is not a passive
but an active condition,
not a negation but an
affirmation. It is a gesture
as strong as war.

MARY ROBERTS RINEHART

*C*ome away from the din.
Come away to the quiet fields,
over which the great sky stretches,
and where, between us
and the stars, there lies

but silence; and there,
in the stillness let us listen
to the voice that is speaking
within us.

JEROME K. JEROME
(1859-1927)

May peace and peace
and peace be everywhere.

THE UPANISHADS
(c. 900-600 BC)

*The quiet mind
is richer than
a crown.
... Such sweet
content, such minds,
such sleep,
such bliss
Beggars enjoy
when princes oft
do miss.*

ROBERT GREENE
(1558–1592)

My greatest wealth
is the deep stillness
in which I strive and grow
and win what the world
cannot take from me
with fire or sword.

JOHANN WOLFGANG VON GOETHE
(1749-1832)

The poor long
for riches and the rich
for heaven, but the wise
long for a state
of tranquillity.

SWAMI RAMA

*U*ltimately we have just
one moral duty: to reclaim
large areas of peace
in ourselves, more and more
peace, and to reflect it
toward others. And the more
peace there is in us, the more
peace there will be in
our troubled world.

ETTY HILLESUM

*P*EACE IS INEVITABLE
TO THOSE WHO OFFER PEACE.

FROM "A COURSE IN MIRACLES"

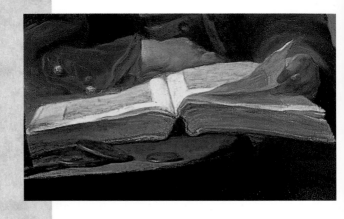

*The strong, calm man
is always loved and revered.
He is like a shade-giving tree
in a thirsty land,
or a sheltering rock
in a storm.*

JAMES ALLEN· (1864-1912)

*FROM SERENITY
COMES
GENTLENESS,
COMES
LASTING STRENGTH.*

PAM BROWN, b.1928

*To a mind
that is still
the whole universe
surrenders.*

CHUANG TZU

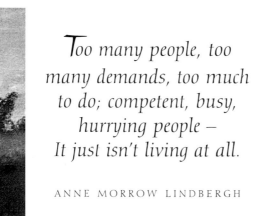

*Too many people, too
many demands, too much
to do; competent, busy,
hurrying people –
It just isn't living at all.*

ANNE MORROW LINDBERGH

*Life is eating us up.
We shall be fables
presently. Keep cool:
it will be all one
a hundred years hence.*

RALPH WALDO EMERSON
(1803–1882)

AND SO, WHILE OTHERS MISERABLY PLEDGE THEMSELVES TO THE INSATIABLE PURSUIT OF AMBITION AND

*BRIEF POWER, I WILL
BE STRETCHED OUT
IN THE SHADE, SINGING.*

FRAY LUIS DE LEÓN (c.1527-1591)

WHAT LIFE CAN COMPARE TO THIS? SITTING QUIETLY BY THE WINDOW, I WATCH THE LEAVES FALL AND THE FLOWERS BLOOM, AS THE SEASONS COME AND GO.

HSUEH-TOU (950-1052)

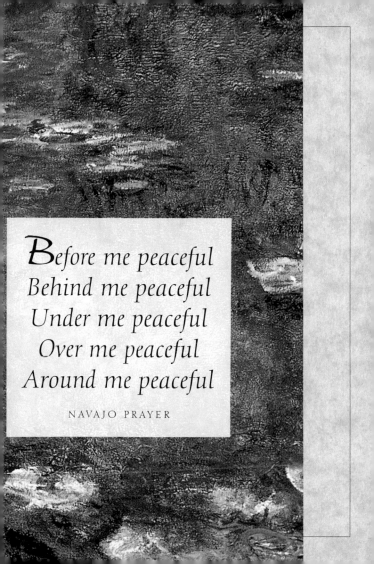

Before me peaceful
Behind me peaceful
Under me peaceful
Over me peaceful
Around me peaceful

NAVAJO PRAYER

Acknowledgements: The publishers are grateful for permission to reproduce copyright material. Whilst every reasonable effort has been made to trace copyright holders, the publishers would be pleased to hear from any not here acknowledged. THICH NHAT HANH: From *Being Peace* (1987) by Thich Nhat Hanh with permission from Parallax Press, Berkeley, California. ETTY HILLESUM: From *An Interrupted Life – The Diaries of Etty Hillesum 1941-1943.* ANNE MORROW LINDBERGH: From *Bring Me A Unicorn,* published by Harcourt Brace Jovanovich, 1971, 1972 by Anne Morrow Lindbergh. J. DONALD WALTERS: From *"There's Joy in the Heavens",* published by Crystal Clarity Publishers.

Picture credits: Exley Publications would like to thank the following organizations and individuals for permission to reproduce their pictures. Whilst every reasonable effort has been made to trace the copyright holders, the publishers would be pleased to hear from any not here acknowledged. Archiv für Kunst (AKG), Artworks (AW), Bridgeman Art Library (BAL), Fine Art Photographic Library (FAP), Giraudon (GIR), Index (IND), SuperStock (SS). Cover and title page: Claude Monet, *Waterlilies;* pages 6/7: Valentin Alexandrovitch Serov, *Pond in Thicket,* AKG; pages 8/9: © 1998 Walter Farmer, *Through a Window,* BAL; page 10: Norbert Goeneutte, *Doctor Paul Gachet,* GIR; page 12: Matias Morales, *Columbian Woman on a Divan,* SS; page 14: Gamaliel Subang, *Dining Table;* page 16: © 1998 Florence Eden, *The Little Weaver,* SS; page 19:

Aleksandr Andreevic Ivanov, *Water and Stones,* SS; page 21: Edouard Dubufe, *Portrait of Juliette Dubufe,* GIR; page 23: Eugene Boudin, *Trouville: The Pier,* GIR; pages 24/25: Pierre Auguste Renoir, *Summer Landscape,* BAL; page 26: Karoly Ferenczy, *Bird Song,* BAL; page 29: © 1998 Harold Speed, *The Garden Path,* SS; page 30: James Jacques Joseph Tissot, *Reverie: Mrs Newton Reclining in a Chair,* BAL; page 33: Berga I. Boix, *Countryside,* IND; pages 34/35: Elliot Clark, *Cold Spring Harbor;* page 37: Jean Hippolyle Flandrin, *Nude Young Man At The Seaside,* GIR; page 39: © 1998 Gyokudo Kawai, *Summer Shower,* BAL; pages 40/41: Timothy Easton, *Morning Break,* BAL; page 43: © 1998 Karen Armitage, *Agapanthus Molucela Arrangement in a Glass Vase,* BAL; page 44: John Atkinson Grimshaw, *Moonlight on the Lake, Roundhay Park,* FAP; page 47: *Home Sweet Home;* page 48: 1998 Juan Lascano, *Baskets of Bread,* SS; page 50: Paul Cezanne, *The Bridge At Maincy,* GIR/BAL; pages 52/53: Adelsteen Normann, *Reflections in a Norwegian Fjord,* FAP; page 55: © 1998 Charles Neal, *River Nene,* SS; page 56: © 1998 Dame Laura Knight, *Summertime, Cornwall,* BAL; pages 58/59: John Ruskin, *Stormy Sunset,* BAL; pages 60/61: John Hollis Kaufmann, *Sea Change,* SS; page 62: © 1998 Rose Mary Barton, *The Haycart Approaches,* BAL; page 65: © 1998 Joel Spector, AW; page 66: J.S. Chardin, *Portrait of Jacques Aved,* GIR; page 68: Private Collection; pages 70/71: Vincent Van Gogh, *Garden of Daubigny;* page 73: © 1998 Alberto Pisa, *Holmwood, Surrey,* BAL; pages 74/75: Claude Monet, *Waterlilies.*

*All children have
a strong desire to read
to themselves...*
*and a sense of achievement when they can do so.
The* **read it yourself** *series has been devised to
satisfy their desire, and to give them that sense
of achievement. The series is graded for specific
reading ages, using simple vocabulary and
sentence structure, and the illustrations
complement the text so that the words and
pictures together form an integrated whole.*

LADYBIRD BOOKS, INC.
Lewiston, Maine 04240 U.S.A.
© LADYBIRD BOOKS LTD MCMLXXVIII
Loughborough, Leicestershire, England

Printed in England

Robinson Crusoe

adapted by Fran Hunia
from Daniel Defoe's original story
illustrated by Robert Ayton

Ladybird Books

When Robinson Crusoe was a boy, he wanted to go to sea. His parents would not let him go.

"There are so many dangers at sea," they said. "Stay here with us. You will have more fun here."

Many years went by. At last Robinson Crusoe was a man. Again he asked his parents to let him go to sea. Again his parents said, "No. You must stay here with us."

By now Robinson Crusoe was tired of waiting. He ran away with a friend and went to sea on a big ship.

Robinson Crusoe was happy at sea. He liked the work, and he made some good friends on the ship.

Then one afternoon there was a storm. Big waves crashed against the ship, and Robinson Crusoe

remembered all the dangers his parents had talked about. He was sorry he had run away from home.

"After this, I will go home and stay there," he said to himself. "I will not go to sea again."

Then there was a *crash!* A big
wave came up and pulled
Robinson Crusoe off the ship and
into the water.

It was a good thing he could
swim! He could not see where he
was going, but he swam on and on.

At last he came to an island.
Tired out, he walked up the beach
to get away from the big waves.

Then he pulled himself up into
a tree and stayed there all night.

③

When the sun came up the next day, Robinson Crusoe jumped down from the tree and went to look for the other men from the ship.

He looked on the beach and in the trees, but he could not see anyone. He called out again and again, but no one was there.

Robinson Crusoe looked out to sea and saw the ship that he had been on. He swam out to it to look for his friends. He called and called, but no one was there.

Then he saw the ship's dog and two cats. He was pleased to have some friends at last.

"You can come to my island with me," he said.

As he looked around the ship, Robinson Crusoe saw many other things that he wanted to take to the island with him. He had to make a raft to hold everything. Then he called to the dog and the cats, and off they all went to the island.

It was hard work for Robinson Crusoe, but the dog and the cats liked it!

Robinson Crusoe wanted to go
out to the ship again the next
day, but that night the storm
came up again.

There was a *crash!* Robinson Crusoe looked up and saw his ship go down into the water.

He was sorry to see it go, but glad that he had taken so many of the things he wanted from it.

Now that the ship was gone, Robinson Crusoe knew that he would have to stay on the island.

"I must get to work and build a good house," he said to himself. "I will build it on top of the hill, so that I can look out to sea."

Robinson Crusoe cut down some big trees to make his house. He worked hard for days and days, and at last it was ready.

Robinson Crusoe was pleased with his house.

"Now I can sit by my window and see when a ship comes," he said. "But how can I let the ship know that I am here? I will have to make a fire to signal to it."

Robinson Crusoe went down to the beach to make his signal fire.

His dog helped him. Now all he had to do was light the fire when he saw a ship.

I came ashore here September 30th 1659

By now Robinson Crusoe had been on the island for days and days.

"I must make a calendar to help me remember how long I have been here," he said. "I will get a big stick and put one cut on it each day. Then I can look at it and count how many days I have been here."

Robinson Crusoe put his calendar on the beach. It looked funny, but it worked, and he was pleased with it.

One day Robinson Crusoe wanted to have a good look at his island. He went off, with his dog running after him.

He looked down the beach and saw some goats.

"Goats give milk," he said to himself, "and milk is one of the things I want. I must get some goats and keep them by my house on the hill. But how can I catch them? It will be hard work!"

It *was* hard work!

All that day, Robinson Crusoe and his dog ran up and down the beach after the goats.

Robinson Crusoe was soon tired, but he would not give up. At last he had some goats to take home with him. There was one big goat and two little ones.

He was pleased with his day's work. Now he would have all the milk he wanted.

As the years went by, Robinson Crusoe's clothes became more and more ragged. He had to make himself some new clothes from goat skins. He also made an umbrella, to keep the sun off him as he worked.

He was pleased with his new clothes and his umbrella.

Robinson Crusoe was working near his house one day, when he picked up a bag that he had taken from the ship. Some grains of wheat fell out of the bag.

A few days later, Robinson Crusoe saw something growing. He remembered the bag and the wheat that had fallen out.

"This must be wheat that is growing here," he said. "I will water it and take care of it. It would be good to have some wheat to make into bread."

Robinson Crusoe made some pots to keep his wheat in. He was so pleased with them that he made some more to put his goat's milk in. But the milk ran out the bottom of the pots.

Then Robinson Crusoe remembered the pots he had made at school when he was a boy. He remembered that they had to be "fired" to make them hard.

He made a big fire and put some of his pots in it. He worked all day and all night to keep the fire going.

The next day he pulled the pots out of the fire with a stick. He put some milk in the fired pots. The milk stayed in.

Robinson Crusoe was very pleased with himself!

One afternoon Robinson Crusoe
was out watering his wheat. He
looked up and saw a ship! He fired
his gun, and ran to light his signal
fire. Then he waited on the beach
for the ship to come and get him.

But no one on the ship saw the
signals. Robinson Crusoe called
out and waved, but it was no use.
The ship went by.

By now Robinson Crusoe had been on the island for many years. He had goats and wheat and a good house, but he had no one to talk to. He wanted to get away from the island.

''I must make a boat to take me away from here,'' he said.

Robinson Crusoe looked for the biggest tree on the island. He cut it down to make it into a boat.

It was hard work, but at last the boat was ready. Robinson Crusoe pulled and pulled, but the boat was too big and heavy. He could not get it down to the beach.

One day, when Robinson Crusoe was walking on the beach, he saw a footprint. He knew it was not *his* footprint, because it was too big. He looked around.

"Who could have made this footprint?" he asked. "There must be someone else here on my island. I will have to look and see who it is."

Robinson Crusoe looked up and down the beach to see who had made the footprint. Then he saw some men with little boats down by the water.

One man was running away from the others. He ran to Robinson Crusoe, and the other men ran after him.

"I must help that man," Robinson Crusoe said to himself.

Robinson Crusoe said to the man, "Come with me. I will help you."

Then he fired his gun, and the other men ran off.

Robinson Crusoe was glad to have a friend again.

"Today is Friday," he said, "so I will call you Friday. Come on, I will take you to see my house and my island. You can stay here with me for as long as you like."

Friday went home with Robinson Crusoe. He liked the house and was happy to stay there. He helped Robinson Crusoe milk the goats, water the wheat, and make the bread.

Robinson Crusoe was pleased to have a friend to talk to. He spoke to Friday in English, and soon Friday could speak English, too.

One day Friday was on the beach and Robinson Crusoe was working near the house. Friday came running up from the beach.

"Robinson, Robinson," he called. "Come, come. Big, big boat."

Robinson Crusoe looked out to sea. Yes, there was a ship coming.

Robinson Crusoe ran down to the beach, calling and waving as he went. He lit a fire to signal the ship.

The captain saw the signal and stopped the ship. He let a boat down into the water, and went to see what Robinson Crusoe wanted.

The captain of the ship was English. He said he would take Robinson Crusoe and Friday home with him.

They thanked the captain and went to get the things they wanted to take on the ship with them.

I came ashore here September 30th 1659

Robinson Crusoe was pleased to be going home at last, but he was sorry to leave his house, his goats, his wheat, and the island that had been his home for so many years.